The Complete History of Toronto Maple Leafs Championships

in the Last ~~Five~~ Six Decades

Stan Lee Slump

The Complete History of Toronto Maple Leafs
Championships in the Last Six Decades

This book is available in quantity at a discount
for your group or organization or as a fundraiser.

For further information, contact the publisher at: info@TenStarPublishing.com

Published 2021 by Ten Star Publishing Ltd

ISBN: 978-1-7778712-0-8

Book, cover design and text by Stan Lee Slump

www.StanSlump.com

Find Stan Lee Slump on Twitter and Instagram @StanSlump or

email Stan Lee Slump at Stan@StanSlump.com.

Praise for Stan Lee Slump's *Complete History of Toronto Maple Leafs Championships*

"For fans young and old, this book is an exciting way to learn about Toronto hockey history. Slump has crafted a must-read."

- J.T. - history professor

"*The Complete History* vividly captures all the Stanley Cup championships as if you were there."

- D.P. - student, sports media

"Fascinating and informative reading. Slump's updates and revisions are solidly researched. The result is serious scholarship about a Toronto hockey team that is followed by fans near and far."

- M.S. - documentary producer

"Thoroughly researched by Slump. A real page turner."

- W.C. - hockey scholar

"Before Slump, there was nothing available to reminisce about past Stanley Cup championships in Toronto. Slump has filled that void."

- R.V. - Maple Leafs fan since 1932

"*The Complete History* was so entertaining, I read it twice."

- D.S. - Maple Leafs fan since 1968

About the Author

Stan Lee Slump was born in 1971 and holds an M.A. in Sports History from Harvard. He is an author, editor, researcher, lecturer, and sports historian, president of the International Society of Sports Annalists, and founding member of the Slump Federation of Sports Writers. His body of work includes research for the internationally acclaimed bestsellers *Wait Till Next Year - The Complete History of Chicago Cubs World Series Championships in the Last Ten Decades* by Billy "The Goat" Slump, and *A Pitch Too Steep - The Complete History of the England National Football Team International Championships in the Last Six Decades* by the Earl of Slump, winner of the 2020 United Kingdom Book Association's Cheap Shot Award. His recent area of interest is the history of professional hockey team dynasties in Toronto, Canada. His first book on this topic, *The Complete History of Toronto Maple Leafs Championships in the Last Five Decades*, has been updated and revised with this new edition.

Find him on social media @StanSlump

www.StanSlump.com

Dedication

To the owners, managers, coaches and players of the past six decades, without whom this book would not have been possible. And to the most dedicated fans in hockey - the Toronto Maple Leafs fans who have steadfastly stood by their team.

Author's Note

I have no words. . . .

Table of Contents

Chapter 1 - The First Decade:

Toronto Maple Leafs Championships

1968-1977

Toronto Maple Leafs Championships 1968-1977

Toronto Maple Leafs Championships 1968-1977

Toronto Maple Leafs Championships 1968-1977

Chapter 2 - The Second Decade:

Toronto Maple Leafs Championships

1978-1987

Toronto Maple Leafs Championships 1978-1987

Toronto Maple Leafs Championships 1978-1987

Toronto Maple Leafs Championships 1978-1987

Chapter 3 - The Third Decade:

Toronto Maple Leafs Championships

1988-1997

Chapter 4 - The Fourth Decade:

Toronto Maple Leafs Championships

1998-2007

Toronto Maple Leafs Championships 1998-2007

Chapter 5 - The Fifth Decade:

Toronto Maple Leafs Championships

2008-2017

Chapter 6 - The Sixth Decade:

Toronto Maple Leafs Championships

2018-present

Toronto Maple Leafs Championships 2018-present

Toronto Maple Leafs Championships 2018-present

Toronto Maple Leafs Championships 2018-present

Toronto Maple Leafs Championships 2018-present

Toronto Maple Leafs Championships 2018-present

Toronto Maple Leafs Championships 2018-present

Toronto Maple Leafs Championships 2018-present

Toronto Maple Leafs Championships 2018-present

Toronto Maple Leafs Championships 2018-present

Toronto Maple Leafs Championships 2018-present

Toronto Maple Leafs Championships 2018-present

Toronto Maple Leafs Championships 2018-present

Toronto Maple Leafs Championships 2018-present

Toronto Maple Leafs Championships 2018-present

Toronto Maple Leafs Championships 2018-present

Toronto Maple Leafs Championships 2018-present

Toronto Maple Leafs Championships 2018-present

Toronto Maple Leafs Championships 2018-present